AN EMPTY SPACE
IN YOUR HEART

AN EMPTY SPACE IN YOUR HEART

Reflections on the Death of a Sibling or Best Friend

Helen Reichert Lambin

AN EMPTY SPACE IN YOUR HEART
Reflections on the Death of a Sibling or Best Friend
Helen Reichert Lambin

Editing by Gregory F. Augustine Pierce
Cover and text design and typesetting by Andrea Reider

Published by ACTA Publications, 4848 N. Clark Street, Chicago, IL 60640, (800) 397-2282, www.actapublications.com

ISBN: 978-0-87946-711-1

Printed in the United States of America by Total Printing Systems
Year 30 29 28 27 26 25 24 23 22 21
Printing 10 9 8 7 6 5 4 3 2 First
Text printed on 30% post-consumer recycled paper

CONTENTS

CONTENTS

Growing Old Without You 31

Of Things Seen/Unseen 45

CONTENTS

On the Block and In the Book   63

Estrangement and Redemption   83

Exit Excess   93

CONTENTS

Pathways Waiting   105

Prayer Possibilities   119

CONTENTS

All Those Memories 131

Home 139

DEDICATION

To those who have passed: my parents, Verto and Helen; my older sisters, Vera and Muriel; and my beloved husband and best friend, Henry J. Lambin.

To those present in the present: our children, Joe, Rosemary, and Jeanne, and those they love, Suzette, Skip, Scott, and granddaughter Jessica; and to my brother-in-spirit, Michael.

To Rosemary especially, who works with me re-reading and revising my writings before they ever leave home.

And to the readers who share the experience of an empty space in their heart, whether it is for a sibling, friend, or animal companion.

INTRODUCTION

Mary came to where Jesus was waiting and fell at his feet, saying,
"Master, if only you had been here, my brother would not have died."
When Jesus saw her sobbing and Jews with her sobbing,
a deep anger welled up within him.
He said, "Where have you put him?"
"Master, come and see," they said.
Now Jesus wept.

Gospel of John 11:32-35 *The Message*

Who knows better the meaning of a particular loss of a loved one than the person who is left behind to grieve? I learned this lesson when my husband of 33-plus years, Henry Lambin, died suddenly of a dissecting aortal aneurysm. I had no time to prepare for his death. Our children and friends and church offered me great comfort, but I still had a loss that I had to deal with personally and in many ways on my own. I received my greatest solace, however, when I eventually wrote and published a book I titled simply *The Death of a Husband*. It wasn't a biography of him nor an autobiography of our marriage. And it wasn't aimed at me, a book with one reader so to speak. It was aimed at all the other women who have lost a husband. I cannot count how many survivors have come up to me after reading that book and said, "Thank you for writing it. I felt it was about my loss as well as yours." Over time I learned that the book also spoke to anyone who had lost a beloved spouse or partner, including both heterosexual and same-sex couples.

That is why I have finally written this book as well. Sooner or later, most of us are faced with the death of a cherished sibling and/or best friend. The distinction between the two is not always clear and distinct. Some siblings are our best friends, some of our best friends are like a brother or sister to us. So whatever category you feel applies to the person who has died and whom you need to mourn is up to you. Or maybe you are at an age like mine (80 something) when you have multiple best friends and/or siblings you want to remember with fondness.

That's why the title of this book includes both.

The entries in this book are not all auto-biographical—some are, some are not. There are other voices, other situations that have been experienced by others that I include as well, although I have changed the names and some of the details to protect the privacy of those who have shared their stories with me.

As noted throughout this book, the term *sibling and/or best friend* means exactly that, but it may not apply to just one person. It also doesn't apply to the idea of the entourage of all one's "friends" (most especially those with whom most or all of your interaction occurred on social media). Yes, you can be sorry that they died and, yes, you may miss them. But when I say "best friend and/or sibling" I mean a person whose death has left an empty space in the room, at a dinner table, in your heart. These are the very few human beings whom you always thought of when things were going badly, or going extremely well. Someone you talked with all the time and called whenever you had big news or a heartache to share. And they were the ones you knew thought that way about you. Or it may be someone you spoke with only at key moments in your life, but they affected you in profound ways.

Perhaps you were separated by distance, by occupation, by age, by gender, by ethnicity, by religion, or by interests, and yet the friendship the two of you shared survives and shines like a beacon for you.

It's a two-sided coin. On the one side is the terrible sense of loss you know you will carry with you for the rest of your life; but on the other hand is the good luck—the blessing, really—of having shared life with that same someone in the first place.

~

I also have both faith and hope that your relationship with your beloved sibling or best friends survives both of you *really* moving on—to some *where*, to some *time*, in some *dimension of human life* where we are still conscious of one another. I can't prove this, of course. But if I didn't believe and/or hope in it, I don't think I could write this book. It would be too sad to write; it would be too sad to read.

I know *death* means "death." But it does not deserve to be treated as a word that should never be spoken. That's unfair to the deceased, and to the survivors. But words sometimes used as well by the wise are words like *passed, passed on, transition,* and *departed.* And these can be good words because they suggest change, not an ending.

We humans can't prevent the death of a sibling or best friend. But we can decide how we are going to respond. Yes, this is a cliché, but it is a cliché that begins as a search for wisdom and hope and ends with acceptance and even joy. I wish you well on your journey and I trust some of the reflections and stories in this book will help you along the way.

LOVE, LOSS, AND LIVING

What we have once enjoyed we can never lose.
All that we deeply love becomes a part of us.

HELEN KELLER

1. FOR YOU THE BELL TOLLS

ONE...TWO...THREE...FOUR...FIVE...SIX...SEVEN.... On and on the church bell tolls, sounding the symbol of your life... and mine. You were a part of my life for so long, and I a part of yours. But if you ask me, it was not long enough.

Remember the poem we read together by John Donne that one time?

> Therefore, send not to know
> For whom the bell tolls,
> It tolls for thee.

The poet/minister wrote it some 400 years ago, but I think he got it right then, and I think he has it right now. I mean on *this* day. The day of your funeral. I know life has losses. We both do. We are grown-ups. But I could deal with it better if only I could go home afterwards and phone you to tell you about this day, these bells. The problem for me is that this day, these bells, are about *you*.

EIGHT...NINE...TEN...ELEVEN...TWELVE.... So many bells in a lifetime. Church bells, school bells, doorbells, hand bells, temple bells, crossing bells, bells on cats' collars. And, in some places, even bells on cows. Bells on New Year's, ringing out the old year, ringing in the new.

THIRTEEN...FOURTEEN...FIFTEEN...SIXTEEN.... Is it tolling the end? Is it tolling the beginning?

SEVENTEEN...EIGHTEEN...NINETEEN... Yes.

TWENTY...TWENTY-ONE.... Yes. I would say both.

2. UNFAIR SHARE

"It's not fair!" How many people—including you and I—have said that? Of life, of friends, and yes, even of siblings. Stories vary, just like details and situations vary. But the basic opened (or unopened) letter might go something like this.

It's not fair! We were supposed to grow older together! We were supposed to share life to the end!

We shared the same set of parents for their lifetimes. We grew up together. We shared a set of bunk beds together for two whole years. You always took the top bunk because you said I would fall out of bed–again—and could get hurt. Well, OK, I guess that was fair.

You made up all these games we played together. Ok, most were good, and some were great. But you always got to be the tribal chief or royal person or chief knight or lead detective, and I only got to be second-in-command. Second usually out of only the two of us. Now, *that* wasn't fair.

Remember how Uncle Tom would send us all a big box of chocolates at Christmas?

We took turns picking one piece. And you always managed to pick the ones you wanted: chocolate and maple, while I would wind up with too many lemon and jelly. I didn't know how you did it until I found out you cut tiny holes in the right side of the chocolates when nobody was looking so you could tell what was which. *That* wasn't fair either.

There was the year we both tried out for the junior/senior high school play, and I got a part, and you didn't. You went over my lines with me—a lot—to help me memorize them. OK, that was *way more* than fair!

We got to be grown-ups together, and that really worked out well. We were there for each other and the skies were fair. But now, here we are. Or rather, here I am. And here you are not. I don't like it this way. Not one bit. I know you didn't choose the time, but I wish it weren't *now*. But still, wherever you are, I hope you are happy.

That would be only fair.

3. LITTLE B(R)OTHER

Well, to be honest, there was nothing unusual about not particularly wanting a new brother when I was six years old. But bringing home this, *this...boy,* was kind of disappointing. After being told how great it would be, here was somebody that pretty much just lay there in his crib, slept, ate, did some rather disgusting things, cried, and now and then made a kind of sound like a happy dove. Sometimes it was hard to understand the choices my parents made.

The thing was, he grew on me. After a while when I bent over to look at him, he made that cooing noise almost every time. And one morning he smiled. A real smile. At me! And then, after a while, when he could walk pretty well, he kept following me around. That could be pretty annoying, I know, but it was kind of nice too, because the boy clearly thought his sister was somebody special. And before I knew it, the boy wound up being somebody special too. Somebody to talk with, to look after, to laugh with, even to lean on sometimes. He was the mischievous brother, the wise brother, the annoying brother, the kind-hearted brother. My bothersome but beloved baby brother.

That went on for more than thirty years. It would have gone on for another thirty or forty or fifty years, except for the accident. He was gone. Way before me. I had never thought it might work that way. I was only left with the hope that it wasn't too hard for him that "dark and stormy" night—the night I couldn't protect my little brother.

I couldn't say, or wish, that it were me instead. There were other people in my life that loved and relied on me—and I felt the same way about them. I didn't want to be in that churchyard, not yet, not for a long time. But I didn't want my brother there either. Not yet. Not for a long time. Not before me.

4. ANOTHER ANGEL
GETS HER WINGS

She wasn't one of your well-known saints, like Therese or Anne or Bernadette. Not that I could recognize any of them in street clothes anyway. But when she moved her head in a certain way, I caught a glimpse of halo shining away for a moment in the growing dusk as we spoke. But there she was, on *my* park bench late on autumn afternoon.

So many times over all these years, my best friend and I had sat on this very park bench. In all seasons we met there, talking about our classes and other kids in school, later about falling in and out of love, about work and family; and we helped each other feel comforted, acknowledge mistakes, and laugh. Well, I wasn't laughing now—the week after her funeral. Nor did I feel much like having a neighborly chat with whoever this stranger was. Another time, I might have been intrigued by the halo, but not this day, not this week, not this year.

"I'm sorry about your friend," she said, after a moment.

"How did *you* know?" I asked, not in a very friendly or inviting way.

"I saw your face, looking at the trees, as if you were looking for someone. And everybody we care about is in some way a friend, you might say."

"You might," I answered, slightly less belligerently.

"And anyway, I already had some advance information, to be honest," she added. She patted the rather tattered handbag at her side affectionately.

"Huh? Advance information?" I did not like the sound of this.

"Well, you might say I traveled a considerable time and distance to come and be of assistance to you."

"Time and distance?" I said skeptically. It was when she turned her head that I caught another glimpse, just a glimpse, of her softly shining halo.

"Your friend has passed on, she is, as they say, dead and gone."

"Yes," I said irritatingly, "I had figured that much out all on my own." But still, she seemed awfully compelling, albeit in a weird way, for want of other words.

She clasped her hands over her crossed knees. "Now I'm not trying to tell you don't be sad. You have every right to be. And I'm not trying to open some Super-Inter-Everything phone service. I can't. All I can say is that sometimes people we love are still here, even if they're not here. "

"Well, that certainly clarifies things," I said, with a little more humor than I felt.

"You may eventually mean that," she said tart-sweetly and started down the path leading away from the bench. I got up to catch up with her—to ask a question, to see where she was going, or maybe just say thank you, but she had disappeared. Gone. Kaput. Finished.

I sat back down on the bench, "our" bench, and I finally was able to cry the way my friend deserved. The tears were bittersweet.

5. PAINTER'S SKY

Dark gray clouds scudding overhead.
Streaks of pale gray backlit in pale pewter.
Still darker clouds massing in the west.
Outside my window
the few remaining leaves on the bare black tree
tremble in the wind.

If this were a painting
something sad and serious
would be happening below:
The surrender of a weary, straggling army,
or perhaps a churchyard
where a handful of stone figures
stand among ancient, faded graves.

Brooding, heavy, lowering, skies.
Nimbus, cirrus, cumulus....
Come one, come all.
Oddly embracing.
Welcomed and welcoming.

A bright blue-white cloud sky
would be unbearable today.

6. THE VEXATIOUS ANGEL

When I was young and came down with childhood illnesses, my father used to tell me folk tales to pass the time. New, or old and re-told, I loved them all.

Now, there are folk tales and there are folk tales. All folk tales are not created equal. Some wrap hidden truths in colored pencil. Some wrap confusion but hide it well. And some wrap little and badly and they don't usually last too long. The words "folk wisdom" didn't come out of nowhere....

Just outside a small village high in the Swiss Alps lived an elderly brother and sister in general harmony. He had never married and was a contented bachelor. She was widowed and her children were scattered across two continents. So they gave sharing a home together a try, and it lasted fifty years.

Oh, yes, they had their arguments. You can't usually live with people for a half century without arguing. Unless one of you is good at not listening and the other is good at not noticing. And especially if both of you are inclined to give unsolicited opinions that are never welcomed but often reciprocated. But the tiffs for these two siblings rarely last long. One person would say: "I'm sorry. I was being crabby and unreasonable."

And the other would say: "You certainly were."

And then the first one would add: "And I think you were also being crabby and unreasonable."

And the second would respond: "I certainly was." And they would then go drink a cup of hot chocolate by the fireside.

That is, until their most recent argument...and their last. He was going to tell his sister he was sorry that evening, but when he came home from work she was already asleep in her room. He was going to tell her the next morning, but she never awoke from that sleep and now was sleeping in the family plot down the hill. But the brother wasn't sleeping too well up the hill.

It was about a week later that the angel arrived at the door in the middle of small blizzard. She shook the snow off her cloak and rubbed its hands in front of the fire.

"Well," said the angel, turning around to the brother, "that last bit between you two was rather botched up, wasn't it?"

The brother wanted to say: "And what business is it of yours?" But the words never came out. Instead he heard himself saying sadly: "Yes, oh yes."

"Well, what are you going to do about it?" the angel asked.

"Just what do you think I can do about it?" the brother said.

"Don't ask me," the angel said. "I'm a neutral third party here. But I suppose you could start by saying what you meant to say; do the 'I'm sorry, we were both wrong' bit."

"I would if I could," the old man said sadly. "But under the circumstances, this does not appear to be much of an option. On the other hand," he said, brightening, "*You* could probably do it for me, being in a different, uh, position."

"Sorry," the angel said. "That's not in my job description. My advice: Just do it."

"And just what makes you so sure she'll hear it?" the brother asked.

"And just what makes you so sure she won't?" the angel said, putting her cloak back on.

"You are the most vexatious angel I have ever met," the old man said.

"And just how many angels have you met?" the angel asked.

"Well, as of now, one."

"I rest my case," the angel said. "*Au revoir, auf wiedersehen,* ciao," the angel said. (Remember, this was Switzerland.) And then she walked right through the closed door.

The brother thought about it and decided what did he have to lose by following the angel's advice? So he tried it. He made himself a cup of hot chocolate and went to sit by the fireside with his sister.

7. OBITUARY UN-NOTICE

There it is, the Obituary/Death Notice. Date of birth and death, maybe place and cause. Parade of names of parents, spouse/partner, children, grandchildren, brothers and sisters. Some of the above, or maybe all of the above. But one significant name isn't there: yours. Because there isn't an Obituary Category for Best Friends.

It's not that you *want* your name there. Who really wants their name as a supporting player in an obituary? It's just that you *would* like to have some kind of official acknowledgement of what you meant to that person, and what he/she meant to you. You were *the* or at least *a* Best Friend. You were certainly one of the fortunate, faithful few who really knew and loved your friend.

All you want is something, some symbol that stands for what you meant to the lead name in *this* obituary, that you did have a special place, even if not an official familial one. Your name shouldn't appear on the official program, but you were a best-supporting player.

Or, on second thought, maybe you don't need to read about this role. You lived it. With joy, with sorrow, with mutual irritation, with comfort given and comfort drawn, with all the things that go along with being a Best Friend. Or, in fact, ignore the cliché element for just a moment and say it to yourself: the two of you were Best Friends Forever. That is enough notice.

8. SIBLING BFF, OR NOT QUITE

Siblings can be best friends. Sometimes they are not. *Friend* isn't a neatly defined a category like *sibling*. Generally speaking, brothers and/or sisters have to acknowledge you as siblings, whether they like you or not. Best friends, on the other hand, are voluntary. You generally know whether or not you are a sibling, but siblings can't always know whether or not they are best friends with one another.

There are both benefits and challenges of being *non-sibling* best friends. Among the challenges, nostalgia can be a two-edged sword. Siblings tend to have memories that don't include you, although you can feel sort of like an extended family member by hearing the family stories over and over, even if you weren't there. Also, there's the Who's Who. Siblings can be added to or ignored, but never replaced. Best friends can be replaced. It can happen through distance, time, attrition, or the advent of new best friends. Sometimes this can widen the circle; other times it draws exclusionary lines.

On the other hand, being a Best Friend is not only a precious gift received and given; it is also a confidence builder. We choose and are chosen by best friends, rather than the relationship being pre-decided by our parents. Best friends are people who don't have to put up with you but do so voluntarily and are happy to do it because you are you.

9. DO I? I DO!

"*D*o *we? We do!*" This is the repeat refrain from a song composed by folk musician Beck Hanson. You can check out the melody on U-Tube. It is quite a noir song, but it is very haunting and repeats again and again a single phrase in answer to various questions such as: "*Do we ever want to take the low road? Do we ever just want to say we're through? Do we want to lock the door and throw away the key? Do we? We do!*

The melody and refrain keep running through my mind, which is how it wound up here. I didn't attempt to duplicate the singer's gifts of rhyme and rhythm. Instead I just borrowed that refrain because it is a good answer to a lot of questions, including: Do I feel a certain amount of envy of the circle of siblings? Do I ever look at sisters lunching in a restaurant? Do I see them leaning in towards one another, touching one another's arms? Do I ever wish that I were one of them?

Do I? I do.

Do I ever see siblings at a picnic? Sitting at tables in the Forest Preserve or park? Laughing, talking, sharing food, playing games with children, and acting a little like children themselves? Do I envy what they are a part of?

Do I? I do.

Do I listen to people talking about reunions with their siblings—events and places and even travel too? Journeys planned, trips remembered, photos to come? Do I smile and sigh inside and wish I had some of those photos and memories, maybe even some small sibling arguments, to share?

Do I? I do.

Do I resent that fact that they have this and I don't? Do I wish that they were more isolated on bad days like you and me? Of course not. That *would* be petty. But do I wish I had some of what they have?

Do I? I do.

So, I thank Beck Hansen for his words and music. Sometimes you borrow legitimately and gratefully where you can—giving credit where credit is due, of course. Do I? I do.

GROWING OLD
WITHOUT YOU

Grow old along with me!
The best is yet to be,
The last of life, for which the first was made:
Our times are in His hand
Who saith "A whole I planned,
Youth shows but half; trust God: see all, nor be afraid!"

ROBERT BROWNING

10. COMPLAINT DEPARTMENT

Not that I want to nag. I just thought I'd remind you that you didn't keep your part of the bargain. Yes, I know it wasn't your fault. But that never stopped either of us from complaining before when we were in the mood.

I know it wasn't a formal agreement, but I thought we had an understanding. If we were going to grow old gracefully or otherwise, we planned to do it together. Just like we had done so many things for so many years. Instead you go off on your own. OK, so I know you didn't much choice in the matter. A time for living and a time for dying and all that. But neither did I.

I suppose I knew it would happen sometime, you being a little older (notice I said "a little"). Although it could, of course, easily have been me. But I didn't expect *sometime* to be *now*. When things were difficult, we were supposed to be there for each other. When things were happy, we were supposed to be able to celebrate together.

We could mourn together. We could laugh together. And when we weren't sure about things, we spent hours figuring it out.

Some of our best times were in those profoundly inane but superficially profound conversations drawn out over hours or miles or food. A lifetime really. I looked up to you and you looked after me, or was it the other way around?

We could cheer each other up—or bring each other down. We would caution or encourage the other as need be, and we always kept the other's confidences. All right, you did try to read my diary, which luckily I had kept in a kind of code.

Maybe we wouldn't have been able to get together all that often as time when on—what with distance and health challenges over the years. But we could have talked on the phone or e-mailed each other or sent sky writers or carrier pigeons. Something.

You're being still around wouldn't have taken away the pain of other losses, but it could have made them easier to bear. And if you and I had grown really older together—a lot older than it turned out—think what role models on aging we might have become.

Oh, my. Come to think of it, maybe in some ways we are.

11. NO SHOW....

We'll have to get together, we said, the last time we met, which was by accident. Yes, we'll have to get together on some kind of regular plan, we agreed. It had been entirely too long, we said, and it was.

Once upon a time, you and I could talk and talk and talk and talk. And we could trust each other because we knew we could also *not* talk about things. The last time we got together felt different, though, almost strained. Polite, well intentioned, and impersonal—until we both caught on simultaneously and became ourselves. We came up with a sort of half-organized plan about how we were going to go about getting together to take advantage of our renewed opportunity, to appreciate what we once had and still could have. No more putting it off as though there was all the time in the world, we promised.

It turned out, of course, that there wasn't all the time in the world. Not in this world, anyway. I'm so sorry, but you know that. And we both believe we'll get another chance, although you know now much better than I how that works.

Good wishes. Good intentions. Did you look forward to getting together as much as I surely did? Was there even then, in the back of each of our minds, a sense of letting go? I don't know. I hope so.

But still, our friendship was real, and it mattered, and brought its own gifts and growth and the times we needed them. Even at the end—because of all those times we did get together in person, by phone, by written words, or with just glances exchanged—we knew what the other was thinking.

So, as the old song goes, "Thanks for the memories." They'll have to be enough for me.

12. THE TOY SHIP

The toy ship had been in the family for more than 100 years. It was carved from fine wood, with masts and railings and a hull that rested in a rack when it wasn't sailing in a pond, a stream, or a bathtub. The wood was covered with marine varnish and paint. And it had cloth sails that could be raised and lowered by pulling on narrow ropes. Now and then it had to be repaired—a crack filled in, repainted, broken masts and torn sales repaired or replaced. But still it lasted and was passed along happily, if sometimes haphazardly, from brother to brother or sister, then to sons and daughters next in the generational lines. That was the tradition. And with good will, some petty grumbling, and good food shared with each transition, it worked.

It should be going now to still another brother or sister as it had done over many of those 100 years. But now there is a glitch. One sibling didn't want it. "Sorry. But that old thing. Look at it. It should be on the rubbish heap by now. You can't even use it for firewood because of the paint still on it. Its day has come and gone."

The next generation, polite and apologetic, was too busy, on the move, sharing spaces, traveling light. And the sibling who wanted it, who would have cherished it, well, that would-be-cherisher had also come and gone—to the churchyard at the edge of town. So the ship sat there on the kitchen table, a battered reminder of what had been.

Maybe it *was* time for it to be put on the rubbish heap—or at least given a backyard burial marked by a suitable stone. But maybe first the little ship should make one more voyage, a kind of solitary victory lap for the hearts it had once won. So down to the lake the last caretaker went one moonlit autumn night to a deserted beach, crossed the sand, and launched the ship in the shallows. For a while it bobbed about, in and out with the white-capped waves. But then, without warning, a much bigger wave surged in and bore it out further, barely visible among the white caps on the crest of the waves. And it was carried swiftly out of reach. Well, maybe that was a good thing, too. Even better. In a few moments it would disappear, as forgotten objects usually did, into the distance.

Except that it **didn't**. Instead of growing smaller and smaller and dimmer and dimmer, as it drew nearer the horizon the toy boat grew larger and larger and brighter and its sails filled with wind. If you listened carefully, you could almost hear the faint sound of the ship's bells over the lapping of the waves. If you looked carefully, you could almost make out figures at the railings as the ship moved gracefully over the horizon.

Now the only sound was the sound of the wind picking up and the waves, lapping at the shore. And the moon drifted out from behind the cloud and made a silver-gold path cross the water.

13. DISCONNECTION

Across the miles, the phone rings loud in an empty room. No one answers. He would be surprised if someone did. No one lives there now. Then the answering mechanism picks up, and he hears his sibling's familiar voice. "Hello there. We're in the middle of a paint project now. Please leave a message and we'll get back to you as soon as possible."

There isn't any paint project, and there isn't any "we." But his sister doesn't want to indicate that she lives there alone. Or, rather, she didn't. "Love you, sis," he says in his best gruff bear voice, as he had done so many times, over so many years, and she always laughed when she heard it.

He hangs up. In a week or two the phone will be disconnected. And eventually someone else will live in the house and have a phone with a different number. It will probably be a cell phone; he has been told the phone company is phasing out landlines. His sister never had a cell phone, one in a series of machines with which she had had a love-hate relationship. But she had promised him to use it whenever she was traveling, or at least away from home. Of course, she never did. They buried it with her for her final journey.

Eventually his sister's apartment will come alive again. Maybe the new tenants will plant new flowers in the window boxes to replace her daisies and petunias. The rooms will once again surround voices and smell of herbs and baking bread as they always did when she lived there. Love, she said, always started in the kitchen. But they will be unknown voices and unfamiliar flowers and different herbs and breads.

He puts his phone back on its table. He wonders—or maybe hopes—that somewhere, somehow, his sister hears his last message in a life-filled sort of space and laughs.

14. I WISH....

I wish I had sometimes been more sensitive.
I wish you hadn't sometimes been so bossy.
I wish sometimes I had taken your advice.
I wish I hadn't borrowed your class ring and then lost it.
I wish you hadn't taken my little green radio apart to try to repair it.
I wish I hadn't told you I found your diary,
and said it wasn't all that interesting anyway.

I wish I had thanked you for always doing more than your share
of the housework tasks Mother gave us.

I wish you hadn't said I was too young to hang out with your friends
when they came to our house.
It made for some interesting listening, though.

I wish I hadn't surreptitiously put pepper and mustard in your coffee
that time we had company and you were acting so grown-up.
You drank it anyway, without even changing expression.
I was impressed.

I wish you hadn't always been so sure you were right.
Especially when I was sure I was.

I wish I had your sense of style.
I'm still working on developing my own.

I wish I could draw like you did, free hand and flowing with life.

I wish I could hear one more of your ghost stories.

I wish we hadn't had some of our petty squabbles.
Well, they seem quite a bit pettier now.
I wish we could make up,
without making a big deal of it,
again.

I wish we could do our spontaneous comedy routine again
for Mother.

I wish I had told you straight out
how glad I am that you were, you *are,* my sibling.
Even if you moved on to where I can't follow you
as I always used to.

At least not right away.

OF THINGS SEEN/UNSEEN

There are more things in heaven and earth, Horatio,
than are dreamt of in our philosophy.

WILLIAM SHAKESPEARE, *Hamlet*

15. SUNSET TO THE EAST

When I was growing up in a small town in Iowa, we lived a block west of the neighborhood grammar school. From the kitchen window above the sink, you could see the metallic dome of its roof. In late winter afternoons, I remember, the light in the sky to the east beyond the dome would turn a beautiful silvery rose. It was a reflection, I suppose, of the sunset in the western sky.

What I remember is that for some reason that reflection would fill me with a kind of undefined joy and longing. The joy, I imagine now, was from the sheer loveliness. The longing? I didn't know what it was at thirteen, and I'm not sure I know what it was now. It's still a kind of mystery to me—not in the crime fiction sense, but in the classic spiritual sense.

More than sixty years later, I can still picture that winter rose-colored sky, the western light glowing towards the east on the dome and everything beyond it. As I write this rose-colored reflection, I think maybe I have a partial answer, or rather a response, to the longing.

The historic Rosehill Cemetery in Chicago near where I live has a number of authentic Tiffany windows—windows whose background I heard about when my daughter Jeanne and I went on a cemetery tour. Yes, a cemetery tour, where we learned about some of the people who were buried there, the events associated with them, and about those windows.

The windows, it was explained, were always built facing west. The metaphor or symbolism is that in death we all go through the sunset, passing into growing darkness...but leaving a glow behind us.

About that longing I experienced as a child? It was for something unknown, not for adventure, or travel, or even romance. My childhood longing brought about by the sunset-illuminating-the-east behind it was for something beyond what I knew I wanted as a child, or even later in life knew only from dry words in dry texts. The silvery rose glow I saw was not the sunset but a reflection of the sunset. The longing I felt was for a life well lived.

16. PENNIES FOR/FROM....

"A penny for your thoughts?" Remember that phrase? I heard it first from my Uncle Nate, who used to say it to me with that nice smile of his. Then he'd produce a coin from somewhere in his sleeve.

What is important to me about this memory is that Nate really was interested in what I thought and listened to what I said and responded to what I actually was saying. We kept it up, he and I, even when I was a grown-up. "A penny for your thoughts, Helen."

Uncle Nate had long since passed on, but how many times did he ask that simple question of me? Double digits definitely, maybe a hundred times or more. It was a ritual we shared.

And now Nate is no longer around to say it and produce the penny from his sleeve. How I wish he would ask for my thoughts just one more time! Maybe as a sort of blessing or hail and farewell or promissory note to be redeemed some time in some still unknown future.

One day, not long ago, there it was, a penny on the front steps of my house. A single penny. It was easy to miss, and it almost was. But I saw it and I picked it up. It had traveled some, that penny. It was no longer coppery bright and shiny; more like a deep bronze or topaz, with its date all but unreadable. Still, it was beautiful in its own cent-sible way.

I don't know how it got there. Or where it was before. But I think maybe I know why it found me.

17. OF TIME ON THE RIVER

"Small wonder that water has been a symbol of life forever and a day," the woman said. "Everything that lives and grows needs water." Adjusting her flowered fisherwoman's hat, she seated herself at the other end of the bench beside the river. "Towns and cities always grow up besides lakes and rivers. And by the sea, although you can't drink the sea unless you're the right sort of sea creature, can you?"

The young man nodded, as neutrally and un-encouraging as possible. He didn't want to be rude. But he didn't want to get into conversation, either. Not just a week after he buried his best friend, Gus.

"And then, our bodies are more than ninety percent water," the fisherwoman added. "Although I don't suppose they knew that way back when." She paused. "I'll have to check that out with some people I know."

"You could Google it," he said, in spite of himself.

"Yes, I know. But it's nice to get a personal perspective, isn't it?" She stopped suddenly, seemingly embarrassed, and looked out at the river.

He glanced at the woman, repressing a smile. The man thought to himself, *Wouldn't Gus make his appearance right about now?*

Gus would have noticed her outfit: plaid cuffed pants, a blazing orange vest of some material that had never grown in a field or flock, a tie-dyed turtleneck. Not that Gus himself had been some kind of style icon. He wore clothes for comfort, not fashion. Gus was the prince of plaids and patterns, the king of polyester. One of his favorite outfits was a pair of navy-and-white small-check pants, always worn with a horizontally striped, red-white-blue polo shirt. Gus explained that it worked perfectly well "because it was color coordinated."

"Thinking of a road-and-river trip, are you?" the fisherwoman suddenly asked the young man.

"Not anymore," he said, startled. How could she have known that he and Gus were planning to go on a long-delayed canoe/camping trip just before Gus went off on his own entirely unplanned final journey? Of course she couldn't have known. But seeing someone sitting by a river for an about an hour, unmoving, she might have made a guess.

The wind was picking up now, and white caps rippled on the shining brown of the river, the current and crosscurrents keeping their own pace on their way to the sea. Across the main channel was an island, anchored by trees whose leaves shielded the channel he was sure was on the other side. In winter, with the branches bare, would you be able to see it? In the distance, he heard the toot of an amplified horn, and a double barge, guided by a gleaming white barge-tender, glided into view and moved regally past downriver.

He could go ahead and maybe work out the canoe trip with another friend, or maybe take a guided tour.

"Some people should not travel together," the woman opined out of the blue, "no matter how well they get along otherwise."

Had he said something aloud? "What are you, a mind-reader?" he asked.

"No," she said, after a pause. "Let's just say I'm attuned."

"They say that in the right light, from the right perspective, the Danube turns blue," he said. "Must be something to see."

"Blue Danube, Blue Nile, deep blue sea," she said. "All very nice. But what about other rivers like this here Mississippi? No one ever says 'Blue Mississippi.'"

"Maybe because it's brown," he said.

"Maybe," she said, clearly unconvinced.

"And then there are all those tributaries that make up the river, tiny little streams and rocky little creek beds flowing into little rivers and over dams and through cities and under bridges. But finally they make it to the sea, after all. No matter what they've gone through."

"But does it really matter that they are now just part of something big and anonymous and aren't themselves any longer?" he asked her, really expecting an answer.

"Is that what you think?" A pause. "Hmmm." She adjusted the flowered hat and stood up. "Well, I've got promises to keep and miles to go before I sleep."

"So did Robert Frost," he said, holding out his hand.

She leaned over and shook it. "Yes," she said, "such a nice man."

He wondered if she meant the poet or his friend, Gus.

He heard her footsteps fading away behind him. Time to go himself; it was getting late in the day. He took off his sunglasses to polish the lenses a bit. Maybe he didn't need them now. The light was changing. As it did, so too did the river and its currents, turning now a soft, silvery blue. Across the channel the trees stood dark green above the silver blue.

For just a moment the young man thought he caught a glimpse of bright orange among the dark green of the islands. Downriver the barge tooted again and passed slowly out of sight.

18. ST. FRANCIS AND
THE BIG BANG

I've always liked Saint Francis of Assisi. Well, really, who doesn't? Francis was not one of our all-too-upright, all-too-uptight sort of saints. He called the sun and wind his "brother," the moon and the Earth his "sister." He preached to the sparrows, who supposedly stood and listened in orderly rows. He wrote the beautiful *Canticle of the Sun*. Francis had authority. He had humility. He had empathy.

One of my favorite stories about Francis concerns a young brother in Francis' community who awoke hungry in the middle of the night but felt it would be wrong to eat. Francis, who happened to be wandering about, told the young brother that he, Francis, was hungry. So, would the young brother join him so he wouldn't have to eat alone? I don't know how authentic the story is. It has elements of apocrypha. But it illustrates the type of person Francis was and the way in which he was remembered by his friends. He loved God. He loved people. He loved God's creatures. He loved God's creation.

There are a lot of stories about St. Francis and animals. That's one of the many reasons I like him so much. I've lived with domestic pets—young, medium-age, and old—for more than half a century. My experience, however, does not compare to that of Francis.

Take for example, the Wolf of Gubbio. This was a large, hungry wolf that was terrorizing a village, dining not only on the livestock of some of the inhabitants but also on some of the inhabitants themselves. Plans were made. A trap was set to catch and destroy the wolf. Fortunately for the wolf and the village, enter St. Francis, who got to the wolf first and made a pact with it. He would see that the wolf had food every day, as long as the wolf left the villagers and their livestock alone. Both sides kept the pact, and the wolf wound up as a kind of protector of the village.

St. Francis never heard of the Big Bang Theory. He was born about seven or eight centuries too soon for that. But it seems likely he would have loved it. It would have been his sort of thing. "My cousin the universe," he might have called it.

According to Big Bang theory, we all come from something so infinitesimally small you could barely even call it a "thing." Animals, rocks, stars, sub-atomic particles, galaxies, cats, cars, flowers, weeds, humans, cell phones, deviled eggs, dogs, elephants, mice, monoliths, humans, you name it: All are made up of whatever it was that was contained in the whatever it was singularity before the Big Bang. Well, something like that anyway. Talk about a really extended family!

So how we treat one another matters, brothers and sisters and cousins. Because we all go way back together in a sense—like some thirteen plus billion years. How we treat our fellow creatures and the creation we enjoy matters. St. Francis would probably—well, possibly anyway—encourage us to see it all as our "BFF."

St. Francis could probably comprehend Big Bang theory considerably better than a lot of people today—including certainly me. He already saw our connectedness. Because, the fact is, brothers and sisters and cousins and best friends, we're all in this together. As of now, we can't look around this planet and say, "Well, it's going downhill, let me off at the next interplanetary stop." And even if we could do so, the mere fact of our interconnectedness expands the extended family. A lot.

So it maybe St. Francis' attitude can help us feel better even at the difficult time of the loss of a loved one. It will not—and should not—diminish our sorrow over the loss of our loved ones. But it does mean that at times when we feel most isolated we are not alone and not without meaning and purpose. We are all part of something meaningful, important to some ones or some things.

19. WHEN YOUR BFF
IS UNKNOWN

Sometimes our "best friend forever" is unknown. I know. It was more than half a century ago, but I have never forgotten my unknown BFF.

Picture this. A woman and two toddlers, ages about sixteen months and twenty-eight months—a little blond boy and his younger sister, sometimes taken for his twin. They are in the New York subway system during late morning rush hour. They don't live in the Big Apple. She's there with her husband for a conference. While he's at meetings, she's going sight-seeing with the children.

She thought rush hour would be over, but it isn't. The subway platform is jammed. Trains on either side are rushing by at incredibly short intervals. She's clutching each child's hand on either side. And then, suddenly, she isn't. She's somehow lost the little boy's hand in the crowd. Picture that awful moment. She's looking desperately, with growing despair. The dangers are all too immediately obvious: falling onto the tracks, taken away by a stranger, getting lost forever. She is calling her son's name, over and over, with increasing desperation.

And then, out of the crowd comes a tall Black man, business-suited, obviously on his way to work like everyone else on the platform. But unlike everyone else, he stopped, and he saw what was happening, and he stepped in. He is holding by his hand the little blond lost boy. "I heard you calling," he said, as she took her son's hand amidst sobs of joy and thank-yous. And then the man was gone.

And for more than half a century I have been grateful to that man and thought of him as an angel—or, more accurately—as the best friend forever whose name I'll never know. Because the woman in the subway was me. The little girl was my daughter Rosemary. And the little lost boy was my son Joe, now 50-plus years old, with a daughter of his own.

ON THE BLOCK AND
IN THE BOOK

Lady Wisdom has built her house and furnished her home.
it's supported by seven brown timbers....
Are you confused about life, don't know what's going on?
Come with me, oh come, have dinner with me!

PROVERBS 9:1-5, *The Message*

20. DULCIE'S SISTER

I met the first sister, Dulcie, when I used to walk my dog after work, or occasionally on a weekend. I didn't walk past her house that often; Dulcie didn't live on our neighborhood, but in another very similar urban neighborhood several blocks away. And Tascha (that was my dog then) and I had a regular sort of route. But we would vary it for adventure. Or to avoid a particularly unpleasant little purebred that would come snapping at Tascha and then leap into its cooing owner's arms.

Sometimes when I passed her house with Tascha, Dulcie would be sitting on her front porch, newspaper in hand. It was a nice, old-fashioned sort of porch, and she would come to the wooden rail to say hello. I don't remember exactly how long I knew her. But what I do remember is that there was a kind of old-fashioned elegance and grace about her, like someone out of a happier version of an Edith Wharton novel. And our conversations had a kind of old-fashioned simplicity about them. We spoke of the weather, the flowers, the dog—that sort of thing.

She lived there, she said, with her older sister Flo. I never met the sister. But I heard enough about her in little vignettes that I was sorry I hadn't. Dulcie said she worked part time at a local resale shop. It was green-friendly charity shop where Flo worked as a volunteer. At seventy-five years of age, I hasten to add. Dulcie told me that if Flo couldn't save the world, she at least wanted to embrace it.

Flo also had a wilder side. For example, Dulcie told me this story about her sister. "When we were young, Papa used to have a motor-cycle with a side car. Mama didn't like it much, but she liked Papa, so she didn't say much, except to warn him to be careful some thousand times. He told her he would, about another thousand times. And he was. Sometimes he would take Flo or me for a little ride. Remember, there wasn't nearly as much traffic in those days. And you couldn't easily tip a sidecar. Well, now and then, when Papa was out of town on business and Mama was going to be gone for several hours, Flo would take that motorcycle out herself, wearing these crazy-looking goggles and with me in the sidecar, both of us in leather helmets like something out of a silent film. Other times she would take one of the young men that hung around her hoping to be *her* young man. I know she shouldn't have done it. But she was careful. I'm here to tell the tale. And Flo was one of those people that sort of bubbles, you know."

Sometimes Dulcie would bring Tascha a nice little treat. She said she reminded her of a smaller dog they used to have and weren't supposed to have. It was a dog Flo found on the street in a thunderstorm and carried home wrapped in her coat. "Now you should understand, Helen," Dulcie said, "that Papa and Mama were not all that eager to have a dog. Not at all. But Mama had to go into action when saw that wet dog and wet Flo, and she got them dried off and warmed up and fed some soup. And then Flo hid the dog under a chair, on the basis that she would sort of inform Papa about the dog little by little until he got used to the idea. But when Papa was sitting there reading the paper, he could see the dog's fluffy white tail sticking out from under the chair. And then the rest of the dog came out. And Papa put down his paper, took off his glasses and said: "Oh, girls, you got yourselves a little dog. And guess who used to take his dog everywhere with him—even in a harness in that side-car."

Sometimes Dulcie and I talked about music. We both loved folk and blue grass. And some classical. Both Dulcie and Flo had played the piano, Dulcie told me, and sometimes they still did, although she said they were very amateur players. I wasn't so sure. Now and then when I passed by and the porch was empty but the windows were open I would hear the sound of Chopin or country-western or something totally unknown but sounding really lovely. One time Dulcie did say her sister used to play piano in an offbeat movie theater that showed silent films.

Sometimes I wondered about those long-ago young men who surrounded the two sisters. Did either one of the girls ever marry? Had a chosen one died in one of the wars that ravaged the world or part of it every few years? Or did they maybe have children, nieces, nephews, grandchildren appear during the times—which were most of the time—when I wasn't nearby?

And then, one day when I walked by, the house had that look empty houses have, and there was a "Sold" sign on the front lawn. The neighbor to the west, who was working in his little front garden, had paused for a rest, and I asked him what had happened to Dulcie and Flo.

"Dulcie died suddenly two weeks ago," he said. "It was heart. They found her sitting in her chair on the front porch, with the newspaper on the table and a little dog treat beside it. We're glad she went peaceful-like, but sorry too. She was a good neighbor, that lady."

"What about her sister Flo?" I asked. "Did she decide to move then?" I could well imagine she might, rather than living in the big old house they shared alone.

"What sister?" the neighbor asked.

"Her sister Flo," I said. "The one that lived with her," I added, trying not to sound impatient.

"Flo?" he said. "A sister?" He paused, looking at me somewhat bewildered. "Dulcie didn't have no sister living with her. Not that I ever knew. She lived alone for as long as we've been here. And we've lived here twenty years."

"Oh," I said. "I must have been thinking of someone else."

That was a few decades back. Tascha has long since gone too. I miss her and other pets I loved that have passed on. I hope they are in a nice, peaceful sort of place, waiting to welcome me.

Maybe all dogs do go to heaven, where I assume that Dulcie still gives her treats. I'm sure Dulcie has long since been welcomed into her own well-deserved new home. But I also firmly believe that she was reunited with her sister there too.

21. GOD'S DYSFUNCTIONAL FAMILY

Standing at the white board, the Professor wrote in large block letters: "GOD'S FUNCTIONAL FAMILY. She paused, then added "DYS" before "FUNCTIONAL."

~

STUDENT 1: Just a minute, professor. Did you JUST make that "God's Dysfunctional Family"? What's that supposed to mean?

PROFESSOR: Let's test the hypothesis, in a sense. No, you there, put away that cell phone. I said *test*, not *text*. Consider this. If we are all God's children, we are therefore all brothers and sisters. Sometimes we even call each other that.

STUDENT 2: Among the other things we call one another, Prof! (Murmuring and laughter from the back row.)

PROFESSOR: Apt observation, Nancy. And more to the point, would you say we very often *don't* treat one another that way?

STUDENT 3: Is that a question? Come on, professor, just look at on social media to see how we treat people.

STUDENT 4: Or the campus. Or the city. Or the country. Or the world.

STUDENT 5: Or maybe we should just look inside this room. Do I *seem* like a brother or sister to you?

STUDENT 1: Actually, yes, but unfortunately. (More murmur-laughter.)

PROFESSOR: Very funny, Nick.

STUDENT 7: Yeah, very funny. But not so funny if you had a brother or sister who died. (Momentary silence.) People aren't perfect, and that includes people who aren't around anymore. But it still sucks.

PROFESSOR: Yes. That can complicate mourning. (Pause.) The people we know and lose are not perfect. Which is probably fortunate. And that includes us.

STUDENT 7: Yeah, whatever.

STUDENT 8: OK, yes. Words are said. Or left unsaid.

STUDENT 9: And all those rivalries, old and new. Like repeating eighth grade forever.

STUDENT 10: And riffs or cracks open without us knowing why or without even the chance to close them. Like when my best friend died. (A longer moment of silence.)

PROFESSOR: Yes, hurt feelings can linger. Things should have been different. Things could have been different. Should they? Could they?

STUDENT 2: But this stuff goes way back. Have you ever looked close at the genealogy in *Matthew*, for example?

SEVERAL STUDENTS IN UNISON: What did you say? Matthew who? What genealogy? What is your point here?

STUDENT 2: Well, if you go through the list of names in the *Gospel of Matthew*, there were some really sort of unusual people there. A lot of solid citizens, apparently, but not all; or at least they didn't start out respectable. One cheated his brother out of his inheritance. One was a prostitute and secret spy. One sent a general to the front lines in battle to be killed because he wanted to marry the general's beautiful widow. And this is the Messiah's ancestors we're talking about.

STUDENT 7: Holy holier than thou, man!

PROFESSOR: Good point. If there was an inter-generational family reunion of Jesus' ancestors, think of the flawed people who would have been around the tables. Go look it up for yourselves.

STUDENT 3: So, you could say that from the start God's family was literally dysfunctional.

STUDENT 11 (usually the quietest one): So. We are imperfect people. We love imperfect people. But that doesn't mean we need to be cheated out of mourning our brothers and sisters. Or our best friends. Or of being mourned ourselves. Even if we are dysfunctional people.

PROFESSOR: That's a good place to end today. There's the bell. All of you pass out quietly, please.

~

A few moaned at the ancient joke, but they liked the professor and were prepared to overlook it. It was one of their friendly and functional ways of being part of a dysfunctional family.

22. SOME SIBLINGS
IN *THE BOOK*

B eing a sibling, having siblings, can have its challenges as well as its blessings. Literature is filled with their stories. Take *The Brothers Karamazov* or *Cinderella*. And that is true of Scripture as well. The world was brand-spanking young and already siblings are squabbling in *Genesis,* sometime after their parents were kicked out of Paradise.

Brothers—and sisters—at times play a big part in the Bible.

First off, for example, is the story of Cain and Abel and sibling rivalry writ large, which is definitely not well resolved. Cain kills Abel and becomes a fugitive, identifiable by a mark that will become a symbol—the mark of Cain.

Down the line along come Isaac and his half-brother Ishmael. Isaac's mother Sarah, believing she is barren, sends her maidservant Hagar to Abraham, to bear him a son. She does: Ishmael. But then Sarah herself becomes pregnant, gives birth to Isaac, and wants neither Hagar nor Ishmael around. She sends them off into the desert without food or water. Abraham follows, however, and gives them some survival supplies, and Ishmael founds his own tribe, the Ishmaelites, whom Muslims claim as their own. This time it was the parent, not the siblings, who were the problem.

Next up are Jacob and Esau. Jacob is Isaac's son. With the help of his mother, Rachel, Jacob cheats his older brother out of his inheritance and birthright. Esau is understandably annoyed, and Jacob has to flee for his life. But things begin looking up. Eventually, in spite of past anger and past injustice, the brothers *are* reconciled, with each taking different parts of the land, but well separated from one another. We don't hear any more about Esau after that, only Jacob and his descendants. But things in the biblical sibling world are beginning to look up.

But then there is female sibling rivalry—this time between sisters Leah and Rachel. Jacob falls in love with Rachel at first sight and works seven years for her father Laban for the right to marry her. But come the big day of the wedding, Laban substitutes Leah instead and Joseph has to work another seven years to get Rachel.

Understandably, as it turned out, neither sister was very happy with this arrangement. But eventually Leah, Rachel, and Rachel's maidservant, Zilpah, becomes the mothers of the twelve sons of Jacob who form the Twelve Tribes of Israel, which became a very big thing (see *Genesis* 29-30). The ways of God can be mysterious.

Those twelve boys can't get along either. Joseph appears to be the favorite, always a thing to avoid if you are a parent. (What would have happened if they had all gotten multi-colored coats?) Ten of Joe's siblings decide to get him out of the picture and sell him to a merchant to be carried off to Egypt. (His younger brother Benjamin, who loves Joseph, wants no part of this.) Eventually there is a famine in Israel and the brothers go to Egypt to seek food. Whom do they meet up with but Joseph, now in a position of power himself. After a bit of non-violent payback by Joseph, however, the brothers are all reconciled and go on to form the Twelve Tribes.

And all of these stories are in *one* book of the Bible, i.e., *Genesis!*

Go on to the second book of the Bible, *Exodus*. Here we find another set of brothers, Moses and Aaron. But in this case, instead of competing, they complement and support each other's gifts—at least most of the time. (Let's not forget Aaron's involvement in the incident with the Golden Calf!) But when God called him to a vitally important position of leadership, Moses didn't have any confidence in his speaking ability, so at his request God made his brother Aaron his official spokesperson.

And let's not forget about another of Moses' siblings: Miriam, the older sister of both Moses and Aaron. When his mother, trying to save Moses' life, places Moses in that basket, it is Miriam who follows the basket along the Nile. And when Pharaoh's daughter finds the basket and takes in the baby, Miriam acts again. Careful not to identify herself as the baby's sister, she cleverly volunteers her mother as a wet-nurse, so that Moses is cared for by his own mother—and eventually is adopted by the Egyptian royal family. Miriam is part of the Exodus from Egypt and leads the women in dancing with a tambourine after the Red Sea Crossing. And in this brief passage, she is described as "the prophet Miriam" (see *Exodus* 15:20-21).

It's true that she gets in trouble for sibling rivalry. In *Numbers* she joins Aaron in criticizing Moses. Is he the only one the Lord has spoken through, they ask? Has not Yahweh spoken through them as well?

The Lord is not pleased with their display of jealousy. Miriam is stricken with leprosy and turns white as snow. Aaron is not. But at this point, brotherly love speaks again. Aaron is not secretly relieved it was Miriam who got leprosy, and Moses does not secretly think, well, it serves her right. Instead, both brothers plead to God from the heart for their beloved sister. The Lord hears them, and Miriam is restored to health and rejoins her people. After her death in the wilderness, she is buried at Kadesh (see *Numbers* 20:1). Check out the word *Kadesh* in a dictionary. One of the meanings is "sacred" or "holy" place.

Fast-forward about 800 years into New Testament times. There are apparently at least three sets of brothers among Jesus' twelve disciples. Two sets are noted in the lists of the Twelve in both *Matthew* and *Mark*: Peter and his brother Andrew, and James and John, the sons of Zebedee (see *Matthew* 10:12-16 and *Mark* 3:1-18.) In *the Gospel of John,* Philip brings his brother Nathaniel to meet Jesus and he becomes a disciple as well (see *John* 1:43-51).

In addition, one of the early Church leaders who play a decisive role in the mission to the Gentiles is the James, son of Alpheus. This James, however, is described not as a brother of another disciple, but as the brother of the Lord himself (see *Matthew* 13:55 and *Galatians* 1:19). And finally there is Thomas, labeled Doubting Thomas by later generations, who is described as a Twin, although his brother or sister never make an official appearance (see *John* 11:16).

Sisters appear in the Christian scriptures too. You remember the names Martha and Mary. They evidently shared a home in Bethany and were very good friends with Jesus; he comes to stay at their house. And yes, squabbling breaks out between the (see *Luke* 10:38-41). Jesus addresses their disagreement with kindness, and *that* story ends there.

But it isn't difficult to imagine a much later epilogue of the story—a sort of part of the story that never was a part. Now, one of the two sisters is the survivor, grieving for the sister now passed on. Maybe it's Martha, who keeps herself busy to deal with her sorrow. Or maybe it's Mary, who withdraws to reflect. Or maybe they reverse roles. And Mary busies herself as she remembers Martha doing, or it is Martha who withdraws to reflect.

These same sisters appear in a miracle/sign story in the because they are also the sisters of Lazarus, about whom the shortest sentence in the Bible was written: "Jesus wept." Jesus comes to these three siblings not as a guest but as a life-giver. He goes to the tomb and restores Lazarus, dead now three days, to life.

So it doesn't take much reflection to see that siblings played an important part in the long road to the birth of the Messiah, in a story set at the beginning of time. They were a part of ordinary life... and they were a part of extraordinary life. There is nothing unusual, for example, about two siblings differing about how to prepare and receive a dinner guest. But it becomes quite out of the ordinary when the guest is the Messiah and Son of God.

What do all these sets of siblings signify? One possibility seems to me to be that this procession of siblings marching through the pages of biblical tradition right from the beginning serves to remind us that not only do brothers and sisters matter but that we are *all* supposed to be brothers and sisters in the family of God. Even though a family can be dysfunctional, eventually things have a way of working out, which is why we say "blood is thicker than water."

ESTRANGEMENT
AND REDEMPTION

*I don't believe an accident of birth makes people
   sisters or brothers.
It makes them siblings, gives them mutuality.
Sisterhood and brotherhood is a condition people
   have to work at.*

MAYA ANGELOU

23. DEATH OF A FRIENDSHIP

INVESTIGATION BY THE CHIEF RECORDING ANGEL
REPORT #3,469,892

Was this death of a friendship metaphorical murder? Was it by accident; sheer carelessness; inevitable; preventable; who knows? It certainly wasn't frozen to death by cold enduring anger. Nor did it succumb to the fever of one friend trying to reform the other. It was not shattered; it was not torn neatly or un-neatly in half. Rather, like the old soldier in the song, it just faded away.

But to continue, Your Godship, this friendship wasn't done in by distance. Although distance can really challenge love, it never dooms it. Sometimes it even makes it more appreciated—both more noticed and more missed.

There was the possibility that the death of this particular friend-ship was facilitated by a FRPO (Friend Poacher.) An explanatory note is needed here, Lord. Human poaching of a friend of another does not, of course, apply to anyone who simply wants to become another friend of a person who already has a BFF. It applies only when someone maneuvers to become the new #1 to another person's BFF. "Replace" is the key word here, and I am glad to report that this particular friendship was not poached by anyone. It simply died of neglect.

However, I am pleased, saddened, and bewildered to report, Munificence, that the old friend's passing was properly mourned by the survivor. I am pleased because the death of anything so valuable as true friendship merits mourning. But I am saddened because I don't like to see these creatures-with-bodies sad (what ever made you come up with that idea, anyway, Your Highestness?) And I'm also bewildered because human mourning often appears to be more or less one-sided. Why is it one FBFF (former best friend forever) can grieve the death of a friend and another apparently cannot, or cannot very much, anyway?

Subjects A (the ones who miss a lapsed friend who has died) can cry, but Subjects B seem to go on with their lives with a shrug.

I don't know how to explain it, Almighty. And neither can Subjects A nor Subjects B. Observation of deaths of friendships is difficult, as you know, Good Godness, and direct interviews of A's and B's, are not, of course, allowed by Your Holy Wisdom.

So I guess it is up to each human Subject to grieve the death of a friendship in his or her own way. In this case, nobody seems to have precipitated its passing. It just faded away.

24. LETTER TO AN ESTRANGED LIVING SIBLING OR FRIEND

How could we have *allowed* it to happen that we've grown this far apart? All those years we were so close, and now we barely speak? Are all our good memories in danger of going down the drain because they are tainted by this estrangement now?

We were there for each other. We talked and we listened. We kept each other's confidences. We supported each other when we were down and offered cautionary advice when necessary. We encouraged one another's gifts and hopes. And we made each other laugh.

Now one of us is dying, but we still have time to fix this.

Yes, we really did annoy each other at times. But holding on to that has not served us well, and we can let it go *now*, can't we? Or maybe even that will have to wait until the other is gone.

That will be all right, too, as long as we both can do it then.

25. STRANGER THAN FRICTION

Many Saturday mornings, I used to go to a prayer service at a neighborhood church. You could pray for yourself, for others, for whatever or whomever you thought of or chose to pray for. And if you wished, you could say a first name or mention a need out loud. And one Saturday morning I said your name.

And then, out of the blue, you call for the first time in years. And before I knew it, and before maybe either of us knew it, we were laughing with one another, talking together, and remembering old and not-so-old times.

"I'm so glad to hear from you," I said.

"Are you really?" you asked. You always were such a great one for asking difficult questions.

I didn't say anything about the prayer service. My sense was that it wasn't the time. "Yes" I answered honestly, "I am."

And I was.

Growing older changes some things, or at least requires they be done differently. But still, once again, we had contact, not coldness. And even that precious sound of our joint laughter, unheard in the world for so long.

And then what happens? Not long after that phone call, you up and die. You go where I don't want to follow. Not yet, anyway. But I'm sure you received a warm welcome and are now and then still laughing like we used to.

I'd much rather miss you *this* way. Believe me.

And, yes, I do mean it.

26. REDEMPTION PRAYER

*L*ord, *I really **don't understand** why I have to endure this heart-break again. Someone I loved so much, now lost a second time to me. First, the estrangement, a kind of little death or a death by a thou-sand unattended cuts. An estrangement I never understood, although I know I played my part.*

Why it happened, how it happened, doesn't seem relevant any-more. There wasn't even a sharp break, just a sort of door closing, or maybe a series of doors closing. Until, finally, Lord, there were no more doors to close.

Then it was the sound of silence. I often love the sound of silence. You know that, Lord. It is often so full of meaning. But not this silence, now made final by a real death, the one slamming shut that cannot be undone.

But here is what I can do now, Lord: I can remember.

- A generosity of spirit, gifts of time and encouragement, presents given from the heart.
- Stories told, made up, dreamed, shared.
- Books borrowed and lent and shared and lost.
- Comfort and advice—needed but neither asked for nor unasked for.
- Humor...and irony.
- Being *friends*. Being really, really *good* friends.

As Frank Sinatra sang: "Oh, no, they can't take that away from me."

EXIT EXCESS

I feel like one
Who treads alone
Some banquet-hall deserted,
Whose lights are fled,
Whose garlands dead,
And all but he departed!

THOMAS MOORE, *Oft in the Stilly Night*

27. DOUBLE WHAMMY

One of the side effects of living long enough (or maybe too long?) is losing so many people you love—to time, to space, to death.

For example, I no longer live in the town I grew up in and have not for many decades. Most of the people I knew, grew up with, and liked—or didn't like—have long ago either left behind what Shakespeare called "this mortal coil" or, as in my case, been left behind still encased in coil. Neither was a matter of choice, but of chance.

I am not a good correspondent or caller. It is one of my most regrettable character flaws. I fully intend to call people I cherish, to get in touch by e-mail or snail mail. To say hello, to set something up. Next week. Next month. Frankly, I am so bad at it that I am lucky to have any friends at all. And I am trying to reform, while there's still time.

Because the other part of growing older semi-successfully is that you lose people simply by outliving them. A few, I know, will outlive me. And a few have passed on a long time ago and much too young.

But it is the long-term old friends and relatives who die that are the double whammy: There but for the grace of God go I.

Those we grow old with, whom we cherish and who cherish us, deserve to be mourned. But at the same time, we have to let some part of the cumulative grief go—not the memories, but the sadness. Otherwise, we will miss the present—the present we will surely miss someday.

Thomas Moore's line, *I feel like one who treads alone,* is not intended as a permanent description of us, our situation, our feelings, and our experience. Nor is it new. Moore lived from 1779 to 1852. But it describes those times of bleakness as sometimes only a poet or prophet can. Or only we can.

28. CURSES!

There are just too DAMN many of you. Too DAMN many losses. (Sorry, I didn't mean to use profanity. OK, I actually did. When you're 80-something you get a special dispensation.)

Too many of you I loved have passed on: my beloved spouse, my family members, my many friends (both two and four-footed). You were all people and creatures who left me a legacy of love and an empty space in my heart that can't be filled.

Dad, mother, husband, siblings, pets, friends. Should I name names? You know who you are.

I miss you.

Don't misunderstand. I'm grateful for what you brought into my life. And I sure as HELL (there she goes again!) hope I brought some good into yours. But still, I miss you so much.

Oh, Lord, treat my curses as sweet incense rising and my raised fists as my evening prayer.

Forgive my anger and heal my sorrow.

29. WHEN YOUR BEST FRIEND IS ALSO YOUR BELOVED SPOUSE/PARTNER

When that person I loved so dearly died, I lost two people at once: my spouse and my best friend. Because they were one and the same person, all those many years ago.

For most of my marriage, having a best friend and beloved spouse wrapped up in one was a good thing. A two-for-one package, if you will. There was always so much to share—as well as someone to (mostly) amiably disagree with. But it's tough being the survivor of the loss of a best friend/beloved spouse at once.

Not that I didn't need or want my other friends and family after Henry died. Not that they didn't matter then. It's obvious, isn't it? They did. They do now! But still, there's always been a big gap in the fabric of my life since my husband and best friend died at exactly the same time—because they were exactly the same person.

What was I to do then? Where could I turn? It seems obvious that I should be able to turn to my spouse for comfort when my best friend died. To have his arms around me, to offer me words or silence that embraced, enveloped, and enclosed me. To know that he, my husband, still truly loved me, valued me, and was as sad as I was that my best friend had died. It was obvious, wasn't it? Henry would do that for me.

And it seems obvious that of all the people I could have turned to at the loss of my beloved life partner, it should have been my best friend. To give me a hug, to offer just the right words or silence, to give me a cup of tea, a glass of wine, a plate of spaghetti, a shoulder to lay my head on. To know that he, of all friends, was there for me as no other friend could possibly be. Henry would do that for me.

So, it's 3:20 in the morning, and I'm awake, still waiting for Henry to comfort me.

30. WHAT IF? IF ONLY

You were much too young. You had so much ahead of you in life—this life. You had so much *present*, without even counting the *future*. And you fought so hard for life. Until it became time to let go, and even that you did with grace and courage.

It had looked for a time as if you were winning the battle against cancer. Well, maybe you did win, but as you did everything else, you won in *your* special way. A friend of ours told of attending the funeral of another young person who died of the virus. And, along with the grief and memories and the "Whys?" came the questions of "What if?" And "If only."

But the minister preaching your funeral sermon brought in another perspective: We can only celebrate the life the person lived, because that is the only life that mattered! So...yes. Your life mattered. It mattered to me, and to so many of your young friends. You lived your live fully, in the time you had, with the vitality, integrity, happiness, sadness, humor, compassion, love, and just-being-you that was you. You made a difference, even in a much shorter time than allotted most of us.

At your young age, you could often see the special good things in other people. Well, with some of them even you had to work at it too. And sometimes you had to work at making others, including me, see them too. But you could do that sort of thing, because you were so *human*—not a plaster saint.

And then there's *fair*. Fair? I was going to say, this ain't fair! But if you were here, you would argue that fair is a hard concept to define. Or you might argue that you still are here—in your own way—and that it's not your fault (or God's) that other people aren't aware of your presence, and I certainly wouldn't want to argue with you.

That's another thing I'm going to miss. With you, with your creative perspective, I could look at things in a new way, a different way, when I needed to, or wanted to. You sort of egged me on in this. I wonder whether you're doing it still....

One last thing. It goes without saying how much so many people miss you. But I'll say it anyway: I miss you. And no, I don't think I can completely help thinking what if...and if only....

31. THE NEXT-TO-LAST-ONE STANDING

One of the results of growing older, well, quite a bit older in my case, is that you outlive cherished family members and friends. Eventually you become one of the last ones standing, in some sense. Except that this isn't a competition.

Now, outliving almost everyone else obviously isn't all negative. It can give you more time than most to spend with those you love and to pursue dreams with them.

It can also give you the time you need to answer three old but important questions: 1) Who am I? 2) What am I leaving behind? 3) Who's left after I go?

Here's a quick and admittedly cursory look at what I've been thinking:

Who am I? Among other things, I've discovered I'm on my way to being one of the remaining representatives of my generation. And I ask you, what kind of nonsense is that? There's always supposed to be an older generation ahead of you. For example, while traveling with my husband, children, and mother decades back, I asked if my mother wanted to see a particular historical monument. She responded: *"I am an historical monument."* I thought it was funny at the time. Now I suspect it was also the truth.

What am I leaving behind? How do I want to be remembered? What is my legacy? Not in the sense of property but of person. Is the world any better, even a little, because I was here? Isn't that a horrid thought? The worst part is that the jury is still out on me, and I've still got time to *do* something significant about the state of the world. If I could just figure out something no one else has already done.

Who's left after I go? It's one thing to be center-stage in your own life drama. We all are, in a sense. It's another to discover you are standing on what appears to be an increasingly empty stage. And it's getting lonely on that stage! Except that, actually, the stage isn't all that empty. Sure some, many, even most of the players I know have exited and left this particular venue. But others have not yet made their entrance. The worst that can happen to me, I hope, is that I will be the second-to-the-last-one standing. That gives me some solace, and I'm going with it!

PATHWAYS WAITING

*Life can only **be understood** backwards,
but it must **be lived** forwards.*

SOREN KIERKEGAARD

32. GETTING IT RIGHT

You helped me feel at home.
Did I also do that for you sometimes?
And now?

I suppose *you* are involved in building more stately mansions in the sky, so to speak.

Me? I can't help you with that now. All I can do is pick up the pieces tumbled around the here and now after your death. I almost feel guilty for not grieving enough.

But I can almost hear you: "Now, that doesn't mean you forgot me or will forget me. You can't. You won't. We go back too far and back too wide and back too long. But after you have sat for a while, and reflected, and held the sorrow you feel to your heart, then maybe you can begin to consider some rebuilding. Yes, you can still miss me. You better! After all, wouldn't I have done at least that for you? But do not miss out on paying attention to all the other things that are a part of your extraordinary life."

That's what you might be saying. It sounds like you, doesn't it? I ought to know after all those years we talked and listened to each other. In fact, it was you who taught me to listen and not just wait for my turn to talk. Remember?

So, see, I did listen.

Did I get it right this time?

33. COULDA, WOULDA, SHOULDA

After a sibling's or friend's funeral or memorial service, try communicating with them. I'm not talking about conducting seances or going into a trance. I'm talking about conversations in your own mind with your loved ones that you coulda, woulda, shoulda had with them but didn't—and no longer can—have.

One of the great things about having friends is talking with them about things important to you. But it is good to remind ourselves that our friends want to do the same thing. Time, like pie, should be shared. So if you're talking with the deceased (go ahead, no one will notice), tell them what is going on in your life, but then try to imagine what might be going on in theirs.

Shared interests can be a good start. Interested people tend to be interesting—unless it's obsessive, of course. And sometimes we discover a new interests in ourselves. Share them with your deceased friends, but also remember what they used to be interested in...or imagine what they might be interested in now.

The same holds for values. It doesn't mean your values have to remain identical or never change. The deceased can disagree with you in various areas, and you with them. There are moral absolutes, but every one of our opinions isn't one of them. Try to imagine how your friend or sibling might react, especially now, to what you are thinking. Learn how to discuss and even disagree gracefully and intelligently.

Be yourself with your dead relative or friend. Maybe your more-or-less *better* self, of course, but be *your* self. Sometimes it's tempting to try to become what you think the other person wants to you to be—a sort of mini-him or mini-her—but that doesn't work that well with people who have passed on. We like people with whom we have things in common, but we also like people who bring diversity and different interests and ideas into life. Nobody but a fool really wants an imitation of himself or herself hanging about too much (at least if they make it to heaven).

Give your new relationship time and give it space. Relationships develop at their own pace. Remember, your friend or sibling has an eternity to get it right.

Come to think about it, so do you.

34. A MOMENT OF CONTENMENT

curled up in bed on a winter weekend
dog curled up at your feet or
cat stretched out beside you
book with marker between beckoning pages
cup of tea on the bedside table

or only one or two of the above
but, still, a moment of contentment

daylight muted by coming clouds
trees black-brown un-leaved
surprising city silence
except for the low urban hum

a moment of contentment

tomorrow will be soon enough to pick up
all those bits and pieces of grief
there is, there will be
ample time to grieve

but for the moment
for this moment
a moment of contentment

35. DOING OLD OR NEWISH THINGS WITH YOUR LOVED ONE (IN MIND)

Many of us have experienced another kind of loss: the loss of a particular activity or event associated with a particular person, especially a sibling or special friend, who has died. Along with the other changes death brings, this loss often goes unnoticed by everyone else. Here are a few ideas, which may be useful or not. Pick and choose or, better yet, make up your own list.

1) Learn a new language or revisit one you learned some time back. (Maybe you and your sibling or friend shared this interest but never pursued it.)

2) Visit somewhere you visited with your sibling or friend, perhaps even parts of your own city or town, and pretend you are a tourist in the area enjoying it from a different perspective.

3) Learn an instrument. Maybe one you and your sibling or friend often admired. It doesn't have to be fancy or costly. I've been taking harmonica classes at the folk music school in my city and have participated in occasional class gigs (unpaid of course) at local restaurants and pubs!

4) Travel to places you've never been with a new friend or on your own. Organized tours can be a good way of approaching this in many cases. There are all kinds, with varying amounts of free times and discretionary choices. While on the trip, write a journal addressed to your deceased friend or sibling.

5) Books can be, stay, and become best friends. Read one that you and your sibling or best friend read together or always talked about reading. If you are a devout film buff, do the same with a movie on TV or in a theater.

6) Exercise. There is a theory that people are more apt to do things like exercise or workouts or running if they do it with someone else. Some things you clearly can't easily do on your own: tennis or baseball, for example. But otherwise? It

is great to have an exercise or running partner or partners. But if you don't, try imagining your sibling or friend doing it with you.

7) Look for opportunities to speak now and then with people your sibling or friend found interesting or special during their lifetime. Talk to these people with your loved one in mind.

36. MY KIND OF DAY

Good morning! It's a gray, overcast sky, with darker gray clouds scudding past a pale sun and still darker brooding clouds building in the west. In other words, it's my kind of day. Remember how I always liked days in early autumn? You—you liked those blue skies with the cumulus clouds piled high in creative shapes. We used to look for pictures in them as kids, remember? And then sometimes you'd make up stories about them. Remember "The Great Cloud Ghost?" Or was that one of the stories I was going to do but never got around to because you were leading me on to the next adventure. You made all sorts of things an adventure.

But anyway, this kind of somber Dutch landscape sky is *my* kind of sky, and this is my kind of day. Or it would be my kind of day if it weren't *today*. Today would have been your birthday.

Well, I guess maybe it still is. Death doesn't cancel out life to that extent. Does it? Because *you* lived. I ought to know. We lived a lot of life together, once upon a time, and we celebrated how many birthdays? Never mind. But you *did* make my childhood (and adulthood) fun, weird, and interesting.

So, how do you celebrate *now*, when time isn't time, or at least the way we divided it up here on Earth? I know there are lots of feast days for some of the major saints. But what about all the others, who by now must make up the vast majority? You can't very well share cake. And I can't very well send you a nice, warm, traditional card that speaks of all your wonderful qualities (and completely ignores the annoying ones).

No, you weren't perfect. You had your own mix of virtues and faults, most of them endearing, only a few of them annoying, and the endearing parts include some of the faults, and the annoying part include some of the virtues. Anyway, you and I couldn't hold a grudge. (A good thing, too, since if you hold a grudge you wind up holding it in both hands and don't have much room for much else. That's my bit of philosophy for the day.)

OK, so you're not here to celebrate. No big deal. We usually didn't celebrate our birthdays on the exact day anyway. We celebrated them whenever we could get together, sometimes several days or even weeks and once several months late. And by the way, you missed my birthday this year, too!

Anyway, Happy Birthday. Even if you are not here to celebrate with *me* today, I can still celebrate *you*. And I do, every day of the year.

PRAYER POSSIBILITIES

When you call on me,
when you come to pray to me,
I'll listen.

JEREMIAH 29:12 *The Message*

37. COMPLAINT DISGUISED AS QUESTION

Lord, I have a question for you. I ask you, what am I supposed to do now for the next months or years or decades without her?

Do I sound foolish? Like some six-year-old whining about the brand-new best friend forever not playing with me anymore? Well, maybe that *is* the way I feel—except maybe more so. I'm a grown up, and we were together for decades.

We never stopped being friends. Not after a lot of years, not after occasional arguments, not after going along different paths. We just stretched out our hands farther.

But her hand has gone so far away—into another dimension—that I don't know what I should do, or can do, or even want to do.

It doesn't seem as if her loss should hurt this much. It's not that I didn't see it coming. Nor that the ending wasn't tearfully beautiful.

And of course, there are other friends. Valued friends. It's not like she was the only one. But she was the only one like *her*.

I hear you saying I have a choice. I can bring my hand back to my side—fist tensed tight. Or I can continue to stretch out my hand out like we used to. I know the right answer.

38. SECOND FIDDLE FRIEND

Lord, do you ever get tired of playing "second fiddle" for the human orchestra? Does it ever seem unseemly to you?

When things are going well, look what happens: We—some of us, anyway, and me for sure—speak with you only in passing. We're glad you're there, of course, but we don't make the time to send more than a passing prayer in your direction. How often do we take or make the time to just hang out and chat, virtually or otherwise, with you? Our conversation comes down to a hurried hello.

That is how we humans feel at the death of our siblings or special friends. They are now playing second fiddle in our lives. We can't ring, e-mail, or text a headstone. We can visit a grave, but it certainly feels that the visit is all too one-sided. And that is why we finally turn to you. Because you are still here. And because you are always there—always ready to move up to the main chair for a while.

You feel like turning your back and saying how busy you are, Lord, and that you'll get back to us? Do you sometimes consider conveying the message that it's a little late now to cozy up to you?

Nah! You say: "Are you tired? Worn out? Burned out on religion? Come to me. Get away with me and you'll recover your life" (see *Matthew* 11:28-30, *The Message*).

Well, here I come. Stoke up the music, or just hang out with me in quiet.

You are my First Fiddle Friend today.

39. HAIKU

Lord, I feel hope-lack.
Loss-lost seeking to be found.
That's it for today.

40. COM-PLAINT-IVE PRAYER

I need someone to complain to, Lord. Not for long. Nothing earth-shaking. Just someone to listen without invisible eye rolling who will not make me feel like a petulant crab. Even if maybe I am, a little bit, a crab. At the moment.

I need someone to complain to. Someone who will have a little patience without making that patience obvious.

Someone for whom I'd do the same thing.

In other words, I need a friend like the one I had, the one who just died. And you, Lord, are it.

It's not that I'm looking for some sort of slide-in replacement, like putting new batteries in an old flashlight or a new card in a digital camera. People are not replacement parts, and there is no one—not even you, Lord—who can replace my beloved.

But still, I still need someone to complain to without wishing I hadn't. Someone who can respect my confidence, withhold judgment, and forget me not.

No, my friend will never be forgotten. And I wouldn't want to forget. But I do want to complain just a little, and you're the only one always available.

41. WHO YOU GONNA CALL...?

One of the tag lines of the popular film *Ghostbusters* was the question: "Who you gonna call?" This was regarding people troubled by unwanted presences, not people missing them. But it also applies to the loss of a beloved sibling or best friend. Who you gonna call?

Who do you call when you most need someone to talk to? Someone who cares completely and carefully? Someone who understands and sympathizes? Someone who might disagree with you and may let you know it, but who loves you anyway? And who do you call for no apparent reason at all, except that you want to talk with them?

So, yes, maybe the reason we pray to God in times of profound grief is because there's no one else that can handle it. God may be the only one able to take our grief in stride.

Remember the words of Isaiah: "...Don't be afraid, I've redeemed you. I've called your name. You're mine" (see Isaiah 43:1, *The Message*).

42. A NATIVE AMERICAN PRAYER FOR GRIEVING

Bow to the South, the place of warmth and hospitality. (Pause for a
moment to let it sink in.)
Bow to the East, the place of dawn and beginnings. (Pause.)
Bow to the North, the place of cold and hardship. (Longer pause
needed here.)
Bow to the West, the place of sunset and letting go. (Here too.)
Bow to Our Mother the Earth. (Take your time. No hurry needed
here.)
And finally, reach up and out raise your arms to Our Father, the Sky.

ALL THOSE MEMORIES

All their life in this world and all their adventures had only been the cover and the title page: now at last they were beginning Chapter One of the Great Story which no one on Earth has read, which goes on forever: in which every chapter is better than the one before.

C. S. LEWIS

43. THANKS FOR THE MEMORIES

Once upon a time in a land not far away there was comedian and actor, Bob Hope. His theme song was "Thanks for the Memories," with music by Ralph Rainger and lyrics by Leo Robin. It was quite a lovely song and a lot of people still like it.

There is a tradition that when a beloved sibling or best friend passes on to the next kingdom, a remaining sibling/best friend was supposed to write his or her own version of thanks for the memories.

On the next two pages are what one person remembered about a beloved sibling or best friend. Who wrote this list? I actually don't know. Maybe it was many of us. When did we write it? Maybe we are still adding to it.

~

Thanks for the memories.

- For bedtime stories and borrowed and passed on toys (and clothes).
- For not telling on me when you shouldn't.
- For telling me off when you should.
- For being my sister, my brother, my best friend and keeping at it.
- For the songs you taught me. Including the ones in my heart.
- For not being perfect, which would have been rather annoying.
- For knowing you weren't perfect and admitting it.
- And not expecting me to be.
- But for being really, nice and kind and generally good.
- For being funny. And for thinking I was.
- For giving me that feeling of: Yes, you can.
- For sharing and doing more than your share of chores or tasks, or whatever the word is these days, when I needed the time and freedom.
- For helping keep me grounded in reality.

- For encouraging me to use my imagination. Remember the stories we used to make up?
- For telling me to practice walking tall when I felt the smallest.
- And reminding me to bend so as not to break.
- For listening and laughing and talking and tears.
- For arguments and agreements and knowing we didn't know. For the Irish Travelers' Blessing you and I used to exchange whenever we parted for any length of time. One I didn't get to give you this one last time. So, I'll give it now. *May the road rise up to meet you. May the wind be always at your back. May the sunshine warm upon your face. May the rain fall soft upon your fields. And, until we meet again, may God hold you in the palm of his hand.*
- Yes, I remember. Sometimes you said "*her*" hand, and we'd both giggle.
- And maybe one day, as I begin my final journey, you'll send it on to me.
- In the meantime, thanks for being you!

44. DON'T CRY FOR ME

OK, this is for me, and for you.

I thought it would be easier and simpler—for me, anyway, after writing this book—to write this reflection. I wanted us to have as many days, months, years together as possible, and I guess we did.

Sometimes I thought it would be a little easier for you not to have to worry about me—to know that I am safe and at peace. Maybe by the time you read this I will have gone through so much—illness, financial issues, losses of my own—that there could even be an unstated sense of relief...for me and for you...that I have "passed to my eternal reward" (what a beautiful phrase that really is).

Anyway, I've been looking at pictures of us, taken over years and years. One of my favorites was taken some years back. It must have been one of our many road trips, when we were both still mobile. We look so good. And so happy. Both of us show trust in each other.

Now, now? If I am gone, know that my final road trip is a happy one, and that I feel as good now as I do in the picture. Hold on to that.

HOME

For tho from out our bourne of Time and Place
The flood may bear me far,
I hope to see my Pilot face to face.
When I have crossed the bar.

ALFRED, LORD TENNYSON

45. ARRIVAL

Were they happy to see you when you arrived that dawn?

Or however time is defined and described there—wherever and whatever *there* is?

Was there a welcoming committee? And of whom was it comprised?

Did the journey seem swift? Slow? Scary? Serene? Was it dark-to-light or something as good...or even better?

The important thing now, I guess, is that I know you've arrived.

And come to think of it, it will be nice to have you be art of my welcoming committee.

In due time.

46. THE VEXATIOUS ANGEL
STRIKES ONE LAST TIME

You would think that ordinary, unsaintly people—people like me—would not have to be concerned with these visitations from Vexatious Angels. Well, you would be mistaken.

There I was, minding my own business one winter afternoon at home, quietly reading and quietly brooding. It can be hard not to brood when your long-time best friend died not that long ago.

A firm, light rap on the door was repeated several times, and then an angel, one I identified fairly quickly as the Vexatious Angel, simply walked through it into the room.

"Am I interrupting anything important?" she asked, shaking some snowflakes off her halo and wiping it on one cuff of her shimmering gown. "You don't look any too happy, Helen. I'm sorry you feel so bad."

"Oh, you are, are you?" said. I am often vexatious myself with these creatures.

The angel straightened her halo. "Mind if I sit down? It's been a long day."

"If you can—I mean, if you wish..."

The V.A. sat down in a rocking chair and the chair began to rock, although she did not appear to have her feet on the floor. "You've had a lot of time walking with your friend I know. Good times. Some bad times. Times the friendship seemed stretched a bit; times it was closer than ever. You had a long time."

"A long time?" I blurted, and then I calmed down. "Yes, I guess so. But now it seems so temporary. For that matter, *everything* seems so *temporary*. One-minute things are fine, and then they change overnight."

"Temporary," the Angel repeated, thoughtfully. "That's not a concept I'm familiar with." She began to rock faster. But the rocking chair didn't creak as it usually did. *That's strange,* I thought.

"And the thing is," I said. "I don't suppose I'll ever have another best friend like that."

"No, I don't suppose you ever will," the angel agreed. "Best friends are rather like snowflakes, you know. Each one distinct. But do you mind if I ask you a question?" Rock. Rock. "Have you considered being open to the possibility of a different best friend? Not a replacement. But a filling in and a filling out best friend?"

"Open to the possibility?"" I replied. "For God's sake, you sound like a self-help book."

"Yes, for God's sake. How clever of you," the Angel said, coolly. "You might be right that for God's sake I *am* a sort of self-help book. Now do you mind answering the question?"

"All right," I agreed. "Sure." But maybe I was not so sure. I mean, like why bother? Besides, it felt a little as if I'd be abandoning my best friend, just because, you know....

"How...insular of you," the Angel said, apparently reading my thoughts. "Never mind. Just be open to possibility, OK? Things may surprise you. I can tell you firsthand that your friend wants you to be happy."

Possibly, maybe hopefully, I thought. But for some reason this thought gave me comfort.

The Angel got up from the rocker and began to unfold her wings. "Well, got to fly. That's a kind of in-house joke."

This time the rocker creaked.

Books on Loss and Grief

- *An A-Z Guide to Letting Go; Constructing a New Normal; and Prayers for Difficult Times* by Helen Reichert Lambin
- *Born to Fly: An Infant's Journey to God* by Cindy Claussen
- *Catholic and Mourning a Loss: 5 Challenges and 5 Opportunities for Catholics to Live and Mourn through a Loss* by Mauryeen O'Brien
- *First Tears after the Loss of Your Child* by Linda Anderson
- *An Empty Space in Your Heart: Reflections on the Death of a Sibling or Best Friend* by Helen Reichert Lambin; *Death of a Child* by Elaine Stillwell; *Death of a Husband* by Helen Reichert Lambin, *Death of a Parent* by Delle Chapman; and *Death of a Wife* by Robert Vogt
- *A Gathering of Angels: Seeking Healing after an Infant's Death* by Victoria Leland, Linda Bailey, and Audra Fox-Murphy
- *God Shed His Grace on Thee: Moving Remembrances of 50 American Catholics* compiled by Carol DeChant (also available on CD)

- *Grieving with Mary* by Mary K. Doyle
- *A Healing Year: Daily Meditations for Living with Loss* by Alaric Lewis
- *Hidden Presence: Twelve Blessings That Transformed Sorrow or Loss* compiled by Gregory F. Augustine Pierce
- *Someone Came before You;* and *We Were Gonna Have a Baby, but We Had an Angel Instead* by Pat Schwiebert, illustrated by Taylor Bills
- *Tear Soup: A Recipe for Healing After Loss* by Pat Schweibert and Chuck DeKlyen, illustrated by Taylor Bills (also available in Spanish)
- *To Say a Few Words: Guidelines for Those Offering Words of Remembrance at a Roman Catholic Funeral* by Michael Cymbala

**Available from booksellers or
www.actapublications.com or 800-397-2282**